D&G BUS

CLIFF BEETON

AMBERLEY

First published 2025

Amberley Publishing
The Hill, Stroud
Gloucestershire, GL5 4EP

www.amberley-books.com

ISBN 978 1 3981 2179 9 (print)
ISBN 978 1 3981 2180 5 (ebook)

British Library Cataloguing in Publication Data.
A catalogue record for this book is available from the British Library.

Origination by Amberley Publishing.
Printed in the UK.

Appointed GPSR EU Representative: Easy Access System Europe Oü, 16879218
Address: Mustamäe tee 50, 10621, Tallinn, Estonia
Contact Details: gpsr.requests@easproject.com, +358 40 500 3575

Introduction

Few people would have predicted that when D&G Bus commenced operations with four minibuses working out of the old PMT garage and bus station at Longton in April 1998, twenty-five years later they would be running over 160 buses from five depots encompassing an area from Manchester in the north, Wolverhampton in the south, Buxton in the east and Chester in the west.

By the end of 1998 the fleet had increased to sixteen vehicles, with the initial all-over dark blue livery being replaced by a lighter blue with cream. Four coaches arrived in the early 2000s for use on school contracts but they were soon sold on and from then on only buses were operated. The initial minibuses were gradually replaced by larger vehicles such as Optare Solos and Dennis Darts.

In 2001 Stoke-on-Trent City Council purchased a fleet of brand new low-floor Dennis Darts to operate on its tendered services under the Cityrider brand, with D&G Bus being the first operator.

By 2004 the old depot at Longton was getting too small to accommodate the steadily increasing fleet so a new one was built at Mossfield Road, Adderley Green. A depot was also opened at Crewe with eight vehicles to service tenders won from Cheshire County Council. The first brand new vehicles to be purchased by the company, two Plaxton Pointer-bodied Dennis Darts, also arrived this year.

Choice Travel of Wednesfield was purchased in 2005 but remained a separate business, although their vehicles were repainted into blue and cream and the occasional transfer took place between the two fleets.

A fleet rebrand in 2009 would see the fleet livery changed from blue and cream to two-tone red and this was followed in 2010 by the purchase of Cotes Heath-based RML Travel, which saw D&G Bus take over their commercial bus services around the Potteries along with some vehicles.

The Adderley Green depot along with thirty buses were sold to Arriva Midlands in 2011 and merged with Arriva's existing Wardle Transport operation in the Potteries. The Crewe depot was unaffected and remained with D&G Bus. The following year Arriva Midlands would also purchase the Midland Choice Travel business at Wednesfield.

D&G Bus returned to the Potteries in 2014 with the commercially operated 'Orange One' between Meir and Newcastle to replace withdrawn First Potteries journeys on their route 1 using four buses in a special orange livery. The winning of the 'Plumline' service from Hanley to Trentham also saw council-owned Optare Versas join the fleet at Crewe.

Further commercial work would arrive in January 2015 with the purchase of the Bakerbus services with eight vehicles, initially based on the Cinderhill industrial estate at Longton.

The big news of 2015 was the repurchase of the Wardle Transport operations from Arriva Midlands along with nineteen buses. The former Adderley Green depot, which had been leased to Arriva, was also part of this deal, so the temporary yard at Cinderhill was then closed. Six of the vehicles acquired were original D&G Dennis Darts that had been sold to Arriva back in 2011 but the majority were ex-Arriva London Plaxton Pointer MPD Dennis Darts and three Alexander ALX400-bodied DAF SB250 double deckers. The sole bus service operated by Copelands of Meir, 40 Longton–Fenton, was taken over in December ahead of low-floor buses being required on these services.

April 2016 would see the acquisition of the bus services operated by Routemaster Buses of Crewe along with five buses, all working from the Crewe depot. Even more work would come D&G's way in Cheshire following the collapse of GHA Coaches in July with a small yard at Wincham, near Northwich, opened to work some of these routes.

The next few years were rather more quiet with the main focus being on the replacement of services deregistered by First Potteries. D&G would become the sole provider of services to Brown Edge, Baddeley Green, Park Site, Abbey Hulton and Birches Head.

Julian Peddles Centrebus would purchase Dave Reeves share of D&G Bus in 2019 but it would retain its fleet name and red livery, although Centrebus-liveried vehicles would occasionally be loaned or transferred.

Following rumours circulating around for many months, it was finally announced that D&G Bus would take over the Cannock depot from Arriva Midlands in January 2021, along with the staff and some buses. It would reuse the former Midland Red 'Chaserider' name for these operations. From that date Cannock paintshop would do the repainting for the whole D&G fleet instead of using outside contractors like Salts at Cobridge.

In February 2023 Arriva North West announced that it proposed to close its depots at Winsford and Macclesfield and cease running buses in Winsford, Macclesfield, Northwich and Crewe from 22 April of that year.

D&G stepped into the breach by registering most of the soon to be abandoned routes, some with the help from Cheshire East Council. They had to source many extra buses for these services, with some coming direct from Centrebus. The Arriva depot at Daw Green Macclesfield was also taken over.

A nice gesture was the repainting in September 2023 of ex-Centrebus Enviro 200 504 into North Western Road Car livery to celebrate 100 years of buses in East Cheshire and North Derbyshire. North Western was broken up in 1972 but many of the routes taken over with the Arriva North West garage closures were original North Western routes, albeit with different numbers.

Towards the end of 2023 a new livery was introduced in a similar scheme to that of Centrebus. The D&G red livery was retained but the rear portion of the bus was painted dark blue separated by a yellow diagonal band.

This book is not designed to be a complete history of D&G Bus with photos of every vehicle owned, but a look at the vehicles that I have photographed over the last twenty-five years or so including those that I was driving when working as a part-time driver for the company.

The initial D&G Bus fleet contained only minibuses from a variety of manufacturers and bodybuilders. D513 FAE (No. 17), seen here resting during duties at the old Hanley bus station in the original all-over blue livery, was a Dormobile-bodied Mercedes L608D that had been new to Bristol City Line.

D&G Bus only ever operated one Leyland Swift midibus, Wright Consort-bodied BNZ 6392 (No. 20), seen here outside the original garage at Longton. It didn't last that long in the fleet, being mainly used on school contracts as it was not fitted with a ticket machine. It had been new as F108 WSD to Russel of Strathaven and had thirty-five coach seats.

D&G Bus only ever owned four coaches that were used on schools and swimming baths contracts. Duple 320-bodied Volvo B10M-61 CNZ 2263 (No. 16) is seen outside the former garage at Longton. It was later sold along with the other coaches when the contracts they worked ended and afterwards only buses were operated. It had been new as F277 WAF to Fords of Gunnislake.

Wright Handybus-bodied Dennis Dart M67 HHB (No. 12) is seen here at Newcastle bus station ready to work a 56 from Newcastle to Clayton, Cambridge Drive. It had been new to Rhondda Buses but came via Stagecoach Red & White.

Marshall Capital-bodied Dennis Dart SLF S195 FFM (No. 139), seen here at Newcastle bus station in the original blue and cream livery but without fleet names, was one of a number of former Halton Transport Dennis Darts to work for D&G Bus. It would later be repainted red and reregistered ENZ 2127.

The first Dennis Darts to join the D&G fleet were two East Lancs-bodied examples that had been new to the Metropolitan Police in 1995. LUI 9649 (No. 8) is seen on the Walton Estate at Stone working a 250 back to Longton. This bus had previously worked for Strawberry Buses, St Helens, and was originally N754 OYR.

Plaxton Pointer-bodied Dennis Dart MPD CHZ 8960 (No. 10) was the first brand new bus purchased by D&G Bus in 2004 as DK54 KKY. It is seen here at Newcastle in June 2009 in original condition complete with gold D&G stickers in the front window. It would later receive the D&G Bus red livery, be sold to Arriva, be repurchased from Arriva and renumbered 176, before going full circle and receiving a heritage repaint back into this livery in 2018.

Plaxton Pointer-bodied Dennis Dart MPD JJZ 5248 (No. 112) is seen climbing up Dogcroft Road, Chell Heath, working tendered service 76 between Bradeley and Tunstall sporting a more blue version of the standard livery. It had previously worked at Wednesfield with Midland Choice Travel.

Marshall Capital-bodied Dennis Dart SLF R713 MEW (No. 14) is seen at Newcastle after arriving on an 85A from Crewe. It had been new to Halton Transport, Widnes, and had also worked for D&G Bus with the cherished registration LUI 9633.

East Lancs bodied Dennis Dart FJZ 4196 (No. 54) was unusual in the fact that it had been new to the Metropolitan Police rather than a bus company. It is seen here at Leek bus station working a 106 to Longton, a one-time Berresfords Motors service. It had also run for D&G Bus with its original registration N748 OYR.

Long wheelbase Optare Excel S3 CLA (No. 153) looks very smart in the original blue and cream livery when seen at Newcastle bus station about to work an 85A to Crewe via Keele University. This bus had been new to Classic of Annfield Plain, Northumberland, but had arrived in the D&G Bus fleet with the purchase of Choice Travel in 2006.

Marshall-bodied Dennis Dart M713 WUD (No 133) is seen at Newcastle laying over before working an 85A short working from Newcastle to Madeley. It had been new to Delta Cars Kirkby-in-Ashfield and had also worked for Midland Choice at Wednesfield before arriving at D&G Bus.

The first three Stoke-on-Trent City Council-owned buses for use on the new Cityrider tendered services were Alexander-bodied Dennis Dart SLFs DA51 XTC (No. 29), DA51 XTD (No. 30) and DA51 XTE (No. 31). All three are pictured here opposite the former D&G Bus depot in Longton a day before they entered service in February 2002.

Cityrider liveried Alexander-bodied Dennis Dart SLF DA51 XTC (No. 29) poses for the camera on the car park opposite the former D&G Bus and PMT depot at Longton in February 2002, the day before it entered service. These buses would transform the image of the tendered service network that they would work by replacing high-floor ageing van-derived minibuses.

The brand new low-floor buses allocated to the tendered network by Stoke-on-Trent City Council made it a lot easier for older people to access the vehicles than it would a high-floor van-derived Mercedes minibus. DG52 TYS (No. 14) is seen at Reginal Mitchell Court, a sheltered housing complex, working an 811 to Tunstall Asda shortly after delivery.

Cityrider-liveried DG52 TYP (No. 15) is seen here laying over outside Tunstall Asda after working in on an 811 from Reginald Mitchell Court via Sneyd Green. The entry into service of these vehicles would transform the tendered services run by D&G Bus from the elderly high-floor van-derived minibuses that had previously worked them.

D&G Bus took delivery of all seven Stoke-on-Trent-owned Cityrider-liveried Alexander-bodied Dennis Darts. DG52 TYS (No. 14) is seen at Newcastle after working tendered route 59A from Hanley via the Hospitals. A nice touch was the 'DG' on the registrations of the last four.

As well as operating all the Cityrider-branded Dennis Darts, D&G Bus also took delivery of the majority of the Cityrider-liveried Optare Solos too. The first of the batch, YN53 EMF (No. 1), is seen at Bradeley working tendered service 811 to Hanley via Bradeley Village in September 2003 shortly after being delivered.

Cityrider-liveried Optare Solo YN53 EMK (No. 3) is seen here leaving the old Hanley bus station on tendered service 59A to Newcastle via the Hospitals shortly after entering service in September 2003. It carries the short-lived D&G Coach & Bus fleet names on the side.

Wright Endurance-bodied Volvo B10B P513 UUG (No. 118) was the first full-size bus purchased by D&G Bus to work the 118 Hanley to Buxton service that had recently been given up by First Potteries. It received a special two-tone green livery with 'Buxton Flyer' branding. It even managed to receive fleet number 118!

One of the most impressive buses to ever work for D&G Bus must surely be Optare Tempo MX06 ADV (No. 18), a 40-foot vehicle that had previously worked in the area with Alton Towers Transport on the shuttle bus from Stoke station to Alton Towers. It is seen here at Adderley Green shortly after being repainted into this stunning two-tone green for the 'Buxton Flyer'.

Plaxton Pointer-bodied Dennis Dart SLF P41 MLE (No. 53) was one of only a handful of dual-door buses to work for D&G Bus. It arrived with the takeover of the RML Travel business in 2010 but had been new to Thorpes, London. It is seen at Penkhull working former RML route 41 from Clayton to Birches Head and is still in London red livery with its RML Travel London-style blinds.

Marshall Capital-bodied Dennis Dart SLF S194 FFM (No. 137) is seen leaving the old Hanley bus station deputising for the usual green-liveried 'Buxton Flyer' Optare Tempo on a 118 to Buxton. The bus had been new to Halton Transport but had worked for Midland at Wednesfield before arriving at Adderley Green.

East Lancs-bodied Dennis Dart N748 OYR (No. 6) was unusual in that it had been new to the Metropolitan Police, London, as opposed to a bus service operator. It is seen at Birches Head working former RML Travel service 41 to Hanley despite showing 7 on the blind. It had previously carried the registration FJZ 4196 for a time with D&G Bus.

Three former Strawberry Buses of St Helens Wright Cadet-bodied DAF SB120s arrived into the D&G fleet and were allocated to Crewe and Adderley Green. YJ51 ENE (No. 24) was allocated to Adderley Green and is seen at Greenmoor Avenue, Wedgwood Farm, ready to work back to Hanley. It had been new to Johnsons Excelbus, Henley-in-Arden.

Wright Cadet-bodied DAF SB 120 YJ53 VDM (No. 26) was another of the former Strawberry Buses of St Helens to join the D&G fleet. It is seen here at Congleton working the Sunday tendered service 38 from Crewe to Macclesfield that was operated by Arriva during the week. This bus was also new to Johnsons Excelbus, Henley-in-Arden.

Following the arrival of Optare Tempo MX06 ADV, Wright Endurance-bodied Volvo B10B P513 UUG (No. 118) was repainted out of its green 'Buxton Flyer' livery into the standard D&G red livery and is seen shortly afterwards at Wedgwood Farm Estate ready to work a 19 back to Hanley. It had been new to Keighley & District.

D&G Bus has trialled many different demonstration vehicles over the last twenty-five years. One demonstrator was Alexander Dennis Enviro 200 YX59 BXW seen here at Madeley working an 85A variant back to Crewe from Hanley in October 2009.

Wright Handybus-bodied Dennis Dart M67 HHB (No. 12) is seen at Hollington Drive, Wedgwood Farm Estate, on its way to Hanley on tendered service 19. This bus had been new to Rhondda Buses but came from Stagecoach South Wales.

D&G ran some Optare Excels including short wheelbase example R987 EWU (No. 154) seen here at the Wedgwood Farm Estate ready to work back to Hanley as a 19. It had previously worked for D&G-owned Midland at Wednesfield but had been new to Capital Logistics at Heathrow.

D&G Bus also operated some long wheelbase Optare Excels. One was S3 CLA (No. 153), seen here on the Wedgwood Farm Estate shortly after being repainted into red from the former blue and cream livery. It had been new to Classic Annifield Plain and had previously worked for the Midland operation at Wednesfield.

D&G Bus operated many Dennis Darts with bodywork by many different bodybuilders. Marshall Capital-bodied Dart SLF LUI 9649 (No. 15) is seen here passing through Chell Heath working a 19 from Wedgwood Farm to Hanley. It had been new to Halton Transport as R714 MEW.

D&G Bus operated three Wright Cadet-bodied DAF SB 120s that had previously worked for Strawberry Buses of St Helens. YJ51 ENE (No. 24) is seen here at Sneyd Green working tendered service 19 from Wedgwood Farm to Hanley. It was new to Johnsons Excelbus, Henley-in-Arden.

An interesting loan for D&G Bus was that of Wardle Transport Carlyle-bodied Dennis Dart RLZ 3218, seen here arriving at Newcastle working an 85 from Hanley to Crewe in summer 2009. It had previously been a Carlyle demonstrator registered G141 GOL and had worked locally for Stevensons of Uttoxeter. Wardle Transport would later be purchased by Arriva and so would the D&G Bus Adderley Green depot, but RLZ 3218 had been sold on by then.

Crewe Depot had one evening journey on the 99 that only ran from Congleton to Knypersley. It then ran private all the way back to Crewe. The rest of the former Bakerbus 99 between Biddulph and Congleton was worked from Longton. Plaxton Pointer-bodied Dennis Dart MPD V261 BNV (No. 192) is seen here at Congleton in April 2015.

D&G Bus operated many Dennis Darts with a multitude of different bodywork. One of the more common examples in the fleet was the Plaxton Pointer MPD such as T467 HNH (No. 87), seen in Birches Head on the former RML Travel route 40 between Hanley and Birches Head shortly after it was taken over.

Marshall-bodied Dennis Dart SLF T310 MBU (No. 132) is seen at Birches Head working former RML Travel route 40 to Hanley. This was the only short-bodied twenty-eight-seat example of this vehicle in the D&G Bus fleet. It had been new to Hattons, St Helens.

D&G Bus only ever operated one Alexander ALX200-bodied Dennis Dart SLF. That was EJZ 2291 (No. 30) seen leaving Longton bus station. This bus would later transfer to Arriva with the sale of the Adderley Green depot in May 2015 and would later be repainted into Arriva livery and transferred to Cannock. It had been new to Northumbria Coaches, Ashington.

Following the purchase of the Bakerbus operations and eight buses in January 2015, a small temporary depot was opened on the Cinderhill industrial estate at Longton. Former Bakerbus Wright Streetlite WFs MX60 GWZ (No. 152) in Tates Travel livery and MX60 GXB (No. 153) in Bakerbus livery are seen parked up on 1 February 2015.

Former Bakerbus Wright Streetlite WF MX60 GXC (No. 154) is seen parked outside the main building of the temporary depot at Cinderhill on 1 March 2015. It carries the livery of Tates Travel, a sister company of Bakers that was also owned by Island Fortitude, but has received D&G Bus fleet names and fleet numbers.

Former Transdev Burnley & Pendle Optare Versa YJ57 XWC (No. 159) is still in its former owner's livery but with D&G Bus fleet names and fleet numbers when seen parked at the temporary depot on the Cinderhill industrial estate at Longton on 1 February 2015.

Former Bakerbus Wright Streetlite WF MX11 EGE (No. 155) is seen at Chell Heath working former Bakerbus route 9 in full Bakerbus livery but with D&G Bus fleet names and fleet numbers on Sunday 17 January 2015, a week after D&G Bus had taken over the Bakerbus operations. It had been new to Supertravel Speke.

Existing D&G Bus vehicles also appeared on the former Bakerbus routes too. MCV Evolution-bodied VDL 180 YJ60 GGV (No. 133) is seen at Chell Heath a week after the takeover working a 9 from Biddulph to Hanley.

Strangely only one of the two Bakers Wright Cadet-bodied VDL SB 120s was purchased by D&G Bus with the Bakerbus operations, the other remained with Bakers. YJ54 CEY (No. 144) is seen leaving Bradeley with a 9 from Hanley to Biddulph in full Bakerbus livery and branding for the 9s but with D&G fleet names in April 2015 shortly before being repainted red.

Five Optare Versas arrived shortly before the takeover of the Bakerbus routes in January 2015. Some were initially allocated to the Crewe depot such as YJ57 XWA (No. 157), seen at Keele University working an 85 from Newcastle to Crewe in March 2015 still in Burnley & Pendle Starship livery with D&G fleet names.

Some of the ex Burnley and Pendle Optare Versas remained at Crewe depot until the Adderley Green depot returned to D&G Bus with the purchase of the Arriva Wardle Tranport operation. YJ57 XVZ (No. 160) still carries its former owners livery at Congleton when working a 99 short working to Knypersley in April 2015.

Plaxton Pointer-bodied Dennis Dart MPD CHZ 8960 (No. 10) was the first brand new vehicle purchased by D&G Bus as DG54 KKY in 2004. It is seen at Adderley Green depot a day before it was sold along with the depot operations to Arriva Midlands-owned Wardle Transport.

Marshall Capital-bodied Dennis Dart ENZ 2127 (No. 139) was another of the vehicles to transfer to Arriva Midlands the next day with the sale of the Adderley Green depot. It had previously been S195 FFM and was new to Halton Transport.

A line up of four Plaxton Beaver-bodied Mercedes 810s at Adderley Green depot on the last day of D&G Bus ownership before operations passed to Arriva Midlands. Present were R110 VNT (No. 110), R726 EGD (No. 95), P556 RNE (No. 25) and R211 VNT (No. 111). P556 RNE had arrived with the RML Travel business.

Six brand new Optare Solo SRs were purchased new in 2013 for use at Crewe. The first four were painted in a silver and pink livery for the new 'one1ink' service linking Crewe Buisness Park–Crewe Town Centre–Bentley Motors. The other two were in standard livery. YN13 HND (No. 4) is seen leaving Crewe bus station in April 2014 in the new livery.

D&G Bus purchased three Scania Omnicity buses from Nottingham City Transport that had been used on services to East Midlands Airport so had large luggage pens present. They were repainted but remained internally in original condition. They initially worked for the Midland operation at Wednesfield before transferring to Crewe where they tended to work longer distance services such as YN04 GMU (No. 129), seen leaving Newcastle on the 85B variant to Bridgemere in July 2014.

Another of the trio of Scaina Omnicity buses was YN04 GMX (No. 131), seen here leaving Shelton on an 85 to Crewe despite the blind still showing Hanley in July 2014. All three were later transferred to South Lancs Travel in exchange for four six-month-old Enviro 200s before the sale of South Lancs Transport to Rotala.

D&G Bus was allocated Stoke City Council-owned Optare Versa YJ59 GHH (No 173) after winning a tender to link Penkhull to Hanley and Newcastle on Sundays, so it diverted its 85 Crewe–Hanley service on Sundays via Penkhull and renumbered them 85A. It tended to work on the normal 85 during the week as seen here in Hanley in March 2014.

In 2014 D&G Bus won the Stoke-on-Trent City Council contract for the 'Plumline' route linking Hanley and Trentham Lakes from Wardle Transport. Two council-owned Optare Versas transferred to D&G and were repainted into a new version of the Plumline livery. WT58 SOT (No. 174) is seen in Shelton soon after the change in June 2014.

Before the repurchase of Wardle Transport from Arriva Midlands, D&G Bus only ever owned one double decker, an East Lancs Vyking-bodied Dennis Trident X80 SLT (No. 180) that had been transferred from South Lancs Travel for a college contract at Crewe depot. It is seen here at Goldenhill working an Asda free bus from Alsager to Tunstall in March 2015. It had been new as a Dennis demonstrator as X645 RDA.

The Midland Choice Travel operation at Wednesfield was purchased by D&G Bus in 2006 and renamed Midland, with the buses being repainted into D&G livery. It was run as a separate operation running tendered and commercial services in the West Midlands and south Staffordshire. Marshall Capital-bodied Dennis Dart SLF R869 MCE (No 3869) is seen at Stafford working an 880 to Perton. The bus had been new to Metroline.

There were only ever two double deckers in the Midland fleet. These were two ex-Nottingham City Transport Dennis Tridents with East Lancs Lolyne bodywork primarily for use on route 10 from Wolverhampton to Perton via Compton. W651 SNN (No. 8651) is seen at Compton on its way to Wolverhampton in September 2012 shortly before the sale to Arriva.

Midland operated mainly single deckers such as Plaxton Pointer-bodied Dennis Dart SLF P153 SMW (No. 2153), seen here at Compton working a 10 to Perton in September 2012. The bus had been new to Thamesdown Transport, Swindon. The Midland operation and 61 buses were sold to Arriva Midlands a few weeks later.

Two of the five ex-Burnley and Pendle Optare Versas arrived in the dark cream and blue livery and looked very smart. They initially entered service on the former Bakerbus routes in this livery before being repainted yellow. YJ57 XVV (No. 161) is seen leaving Chell Heath for Hanley shortly before the route was extended to Newcastle and Clayton.

Another view of former Burnley & Pendle Optare Versa YJ57 XVV (No. 161), seen here waiting time in the evening sunshine at Fegg Hayes on its way back to Hanley from Biddulph. It would shortly be repainted yellow and branded for 'The Nines' when the route was extended from Hanley to Clayton Westbury Park.

Ahead of the repurchase of Wardle Transport from Arriva Midlands, all vehicles included in the deal that were still in Arriva aquamarine would be repainted into D&G red livery by Arriva. Alexander ALX400-bodied DAF SB250 X438 FGP is seen before the transfer in D&G red livery but without fleet names at Abbey Hulton working school route 401 on 29 April 2015. The Arriva fleet number 4812 is applied on the windows.

Four Alexander Dennis Enviro 200 single deckers were delivered new to South Lancs Transport in December 2014 but were transferred to D&G Bus ahead of the sale of South Lancs Transport to Rotala in March 2015. All four kept their original fleet numbers with D&G and ran for a while in the blue, white and yellow livery as seen on SL64 JGV (No. 33) here at Adderley Green depot in May 2015.

Alexander Dennis Enviro 200 YX14 RZA (No. 107) was the first brand new Enviro 200 purchased by D&G Bus after it won the Staffordshire County Council contract for the 841 Stafford–Uttoxeter route from Arriva in 2014. Initially the three buses used for the service were outstationed at the former Stevensons depot at Spath but later moved to Longton after the repurchase of Wardle Transport from Arriva. It is seen here laying over at Uttoxeter bus station.

More youthful second-hand buses were introduced into the fleet after the repurchase of Wardle Transport from Arriva Midlands. Alexander Dennis Enviro 200 YX60 DXK (No. 119) is seen here in all-over white livery at Adderley Green depot shortly after arrival in May 2015. It had been new to Stewarts of Grazeley Green.

Three Optare Solos were purchased from Go Goodwins of Eccles in October 2015 for use at Crewe. YJ60 KFF (No. 130) is seen the day after it had arrived from Eccles still in Go Goodwins blue livery complete with the customary air horns on the roof and additional marker lights. It has already had the blinds reprogrammed for all the D&G routes. They were all repainted into D&G red livery shortly afterwards.

Three Alexander ALX400-bodied DAF SB250 double deckers arrived with the repurchase of Wardle Transport from Arriva but they did not last long in the fleet. They were mainly used on Stoke City football services and service 16 between Hanley and Leek. X432 XGP (No. 177) is seen at Longton on its way back to the garage after working football service BS1 to Bradeley.

An agreement was reached before the repurchase of Wardle Transport from Arriva Midlands that any of the twenty-one buses to be included in the deal that were painted in Arriva Acquamarine would be repainted into D&G red livery by Arriva. One such repaint was former Wardle Transport Dennis Dart MPD Y263 YBC (No. 193), seen here at Birches Head.

The agreement with Arriva to repaint any buses that were in Arriva aquamarine into D&G Bus red livery didn't apply to any buses that were in a red-based livery, so Dennis Dart MPD Y259 YBC (No. 198), seen here in the Arriva-style red Wardles livery, was not repainted. It is seen here at Abbey Hulton working a 43 from Hanley to Baddeley Green.

The first brand new buses to arrive in the now enlarged D&G Bus fleet following the repurchase of the Wardle Transport operation and twenty-one buses from Arriva Midlands were two Optare Metrocity single deckers that arrived in November 2015. YJ65 EVP (No. 145) and YJ65 EVR (No. 146) are seen shortly after arrival at Adderley Green depot. Behind is one of the DAF double deckers that they would shortly replace on the Hanley–Leek route.

A final look at brand new Optare Metrocity YJ65 EVP (No. 145), seen here at Adderley Green depot shortly arriving from the Optare factory in plain white livery before going to Salts for repainting into D&G red livery.

The two Optare Metrocity single deckers were delivered new in all-over white livery and were later repainted into D&G red livery at Salts Coachpainters at Cobridge. YJ65 EVR (No. 146) is seen at Adderley Green depot on 22 November 2015 looking immaculate after being repainted. It was kept inside at the depot until the official launch of the new buses on route 16 Hanley–Leek on 1 December 2015.

The Optare Metrocity buses soon settled in on the 16 Hanley to Leek route but also had scheduled workings on the 31 from Leek to Cheadle via Ipstones. YJ65 EVR (No. 146) is seen here at Leek on its way back to the bus station after working in from Cheadle on a 31.

The five former Transdev Burnley & Pendle Optare Versas were all repainted yellow for the relaunch of the former Bakerbus route 9 from Biddulph to Hanley when it was extended to Newcastle and Clayton and branded as 'The Nines'. YJ57 XWA (No. 157) shows off the new image at Fegg Hayes on its way to Biddulph.

Optare Versa YJ57 XWC (No. 159) is seen here leaving Bradeley after receiving a repaint and branding for 'The Nines'. The base yellow livery is a nod to the former Bakerbus livery that was yellow but only ran from Biddulph to Hanley.

A final look at an Optare Versa in 'The Nines' livery. YJ57 XVV (No. 161) is seen waiting time at Chell Heath while working a 9 from Biddulph to Clayton. The original Bakerbus 9 ran just from Biddulph to Hanley. The onwards extension covered Stoke station, Penkhull, Newcastle and Clayton from former route 41.

Alexander Dennis Enviro 200 YX60 DXK (No. 119) was the only Enviro painted into the yellow 'The Nines' livery. The other five buses that were painted up for the service were the ex-Transdev Optare Versas. It is seen here leaving Fegg Hayes on its way to Biddulph in September 2015. It was new to Stewarts, Grazeley Green.

Another view of Alexander Dennis Enviro 200 YX60 DXK (No. 119) seen here picking up passengers at Chell Heath on its way from Biddulph to Clayton Westbury Park. This bus didn't stay long in 'The Nines' livery as it was repainted into orange 1 livery when the route was cut back from Westbury Park to Newcastle and then requiring only five buses.

Following the reduction in frequency of First Potteries Tangerine route 1 Hanley–Meir–Newcastle from every ten minutes to every twenty minutes, D&G Bus introduced a similar replacement service from Newcastle to Meir every twenty minutes as 'The Orange One'. To operate this service three Alexander Enviro 200s and an Optare Solo were purchased and painted in a special orange livery for the route. Enviro 200 SN11 FFU (No. 111) is seen at Meir Square.

Another of the Enviro 200s in 'The Orange One' livery is SN11 FFW (No. 113), seen here when first repainted at Brookwood Drive Meir just about to start the return journey to Newcastle. All three Enviro 200s had been new to Hatts of Salisbury.

Alexander Enviro 200 SN11 FFU (No. 111) shows off its orange livery and 'The Orange One' branding while laying over in Newcastle bus station before heading off back to Weston Coyney and Meir Square.

The fourth vehicle purchased for 'The Orange One' was Optare Solo YJ56 WUV (No. 114). It received the same orange livery and branding as the Enviros and is seen here at Meir Square before setting off for Newcastle.

An interesting arrival at D&G Bus in January 2016 was Alexander Dennis Enviro 200 YX11 CTZ from Whitelaws of Stonehouse.It is seen here at Adderley Green depot shortly after arriving from Scotland and before going to Salts Coachpainters at Cobridge for a repaint.

Interestingly when Alexander Dennis Enviro 200 YX11 CTZ (No. 100) was repainted it received white livery with black D&G fleet names instead of the usual D&G Bus red livery. This was so that it could be hired out to other bus companies if necessary. It is seen here at Bentilee on its way to take up service on football service BS1 to the Britannia Stadium.

D&G Bus acquired three Alexander ALX400-bodied DAF DB250 double deckers with the purchase of Wardle Transport back from Arriva. All were new to Arriva South London. X441 FPG (No. 179) is seen at Westwood High School, Leek, ready to work a 16 to Hanley on 30 June 2015. This was a regular route for the double deckers.

Another of the Alexander ALX400-bodied DAF DB250 double deckers that arrived with the Wardle Transport business was X432 FGP (No. 177), seen here at Adderley Green depot after working the BS1 Stoke City football service from Smallthorne. They were all repainted into D&G red livery by Arriva as part of the deal.

East Lancs Spryte-bodied Dennis Dart JJZ 5291 (No. 117) is seen parked at Adderley Green depot in March 2016 lettered up for the route linking Crewe Business Park to Bentley Motors. It would be the last non-low-floor bus in service with D&G Bus. It was formerly R519 YRP and was new to Harris Bus, West Thurrock, Essex.

Former Strawberry Buses Wright Cadet-bodied DAF SB180 YJ53 VDM (No. 126) is seen parked up at Crewe Cowley Way depot alongside a First Potteries Wright-bodied Scania on 22 May 2015. It was new to Johnsons, Henley-in-Arden.

Only one of the pair of Bakerbus Wright Cadet-boded DAF SB180s joined the D&G Bus fleet with the purchase of the Bakerbus services. YJ54 CEY (No. 144) initially ran in Bakerbus yellow with D&G fleet names but has received a repaint when seen parked at Crewe's Cowley Way depot on 14 May 2015.

Some of the buses acquired with the repurchase of Wardle Transport from Arriva had previously operated for D&G Bus before the original sale to Arriva Midlands in 2011. DG02 WYB (No. 199) was one such bus and is seen here at St Edwards Park, Leek, on a short working of route 16 from Westwood High School, Leek, to Cellarhead Crossroads.

Three Dennis Darts with Plaxton Pointer bodywork were borrowed from Central Buses of Birmingham to work route 42 Crewe–Congleton via Holmes Chapel following the GHA Coaches collapse. They worked with paper stickers in the windscreen to provide route information. EU06 WGM is seen leaving Congleton on 27 July 2016.

Following the collapse of GHA Coaches in July 2016, D&G Bus secured emergency tenders to run the Congleton Town services from Cheshire County Council. Dennis Dart MPD X546 GGO (No. 185) had already been debranded for disposal but was quickly reinstated to cover the extra work. It is seen working a 92 to Congleton at Buglawton Estate devoid of blinds and fleet names on 8 August 2016.

Fifteen Dennis Darts with Plaxton Pointer MPD bodywork joined the fleet when the Wardle Transport operation based at the former D&G depot at Adderley Green was purchased back from Arriva. One was X247 PGT (No. 189), seen here at Penkhull working a 42 to Silverdale. This bus was new to Arriva London.

Plaxton Pointer MPD-bodied Dennis Dart Y254 YBC (No. 196) is another of the former Arriva London buses that arrived in the fleet with the purchase of Wardle Transport from Arriva Midlands in May 2015. It is seen at Bradwell after working a 17 from Hanley. This was a former First Potteries route taken over by D&G Bus.

Plaxton Pointer MPD-bodied Dennis Dart X249 PGT (No. 191) is seen at Abbey Hulton working a 43 from Baddeley Green to Hanley. This is one of a number of abandoned First Potteries routes taken over by D&G Bus.The bus was new to Arriva London.

Following the repurchase of Wardle Transport from Arriva Midlands fifteen more Dennis Darts with Plaxton Pointer MPD bodywork joined the fleet. JJZ 5250 (No. 186) is seen at Congleton working a 94 to Newcastle.This bus originated in the Midland Wednesfield fleet and had worked for D&G Bus previously.

Two MCW Evolution-bodied VDL 180s were delivered new to the Midland operation at Wednesfield to upgrade route 10 Wolverhampton to Perton. They were transferred to D&G Bus at Crewe before the sale of Midland to Arriva in September 2012 and were later transferred to Adderley Green. YJ60 GDK (No. 132) is seen at Fenton about to work Stoke City football service BS1 from Bradeley.

The second of the pair of MCV Evolution-bodied VDL 180s delivered new for the Midland operation at Wednesfield but transferred to D&G at Crewe before the sale of Midland to Arriva was YJ60 GGV (No. 133), seen here at Mossfield Road, Adderley Green, after working Stoke City service BS1 from Bradeley.

Despite being less than six months old when transferred from South Lancs Travel to D&G Bus in May 2015, the batch of four Enviro 200s were soon repainted into fleet livery. SL64 JGF (No. 30) is seen at Mossfield Road, Adderley Green, just up the road from the depot ready to work a Port Vale away fans bus.

Another of the former South Lancs Travel Alexander Dennis Enviro 200s, SL64 JGU (No. 32) is seen outside Fenton Town Hall working on the former Copelands route 40 from Fenton to Longton via Heron Cross in July 2017.

Former South Lancs Travel SL64 JGV (No 33) is seen at Chell Heath working a 9 from Biddulph to Hanley.This route was taken over with the Bakerbus network in January 2015. The bus kept the same fleet number that it had with South Lancs Travel.

Towards the end of its working life at D&G Bus, Plaxton Pointer-bodied Dennis Dart T467 HNH (No. 187) received this promotional livery in blue and white to work a free bus service for the newly rebulit Tesco superstore at Crewe. Pottering back and forth from the bus station to Tesco would be a lot less ardous work than a full duty on a service route. It is seen here at Adderley Green depot.

Two Wright Commander-bodied DAF SB220s arrived into the D&G Bus fleet with the purchase of the bus services of Routemaster Buses, Crewe. They were both new to Fishwicks of Leyland and ran in their livery with D&G fleet names and numbers. They were not at Routemaster Buses long enough to receive a repaint. YJ53 VDT (No. 148) is seen at Crewe depot shortly after arriving.

Five buses arrived at D&G Bus after the purchase of the bus services of Routemaster Buses, Crewe. Included were two East Lancs-bodied Dennis Darts that had been new to Epsom Coaches Quailty Line. Both arrived in Routemaster Buses two-tone green livery as seen here on Pl05 PLO (No. 163) at Adderley Green before being repainted.

Plaxton Centro YJ07 JWD (No 149) was the only Plaxton Centro-bodied VDL SB220 acquired with the bus services of Routemaster Buses, Crewe, in 2016. It was new to Fishwicks of Leyland and never received a repaint into Routemaster Buses livery. It initially worked for D&G in green livery as seen here at Crewe depot.

The sole Plaxton Centro-bodied VDL SB220 that arrived in the fleet with the Routemaster Buses business, YJ07 JWD (No. 149), is seen here at Keele University working an 85 to Crewe and Nantwich shortly after receiving a repaint. This bus would later transfer to Select Bus Services at Penkridge.

Following the withdrawal of the double deckers, the special football services worked for both Stoke City and Port Vale were then operated by single deckers. Plaxton Centro YJ07 JWD (No. 149) is seen outside the Crewe depot at Cowley Way after working an away fans bus for Port Vale FC in July 2016.

Two Wright Commander-bodied DAF SB220s were acquired with the Routemaster Buses business in 2016. YJ53 VDT (No. 148) is seen here after repaint into D&G red at Keele University working 85 Nantwich–Crewe–Newcastle. This route used to be part of the former Crosville C84 Newcastle–Crewe–Chester.

One of the two ex-Routemaster Buses, Crewe, East Lancs-bodied Dennis Darts PL05 PLU (No. 162), is seen at Adderley Green depot shortly after receiving a coat of red paint. The destination blinds are set for route BS1 Stoke City FC–Smallthorne, which is dubious as a full and standing double decker was the norm on this service.

The other former Transdev York Optare Solo, YJ56 YUT (No. 44), is seen here after entering service with D&G Bus still in its York two-tone blue livery but with D&G fleet names and fleet numbers at Newcastle working a 35 from the Westlands. After a short time in D&G red livery it would later receive the 'Orange 1' livery when that route was extended to Silverdale and Wood Lane.

Alexander Dennis Enviro 200 YX14 RZA (No. 107) was the first Enviro 200 purchased new by the company in 2014 to work the 841 Uttoxeter–Stafford service. It is seen here at Adderley Green depot two years later receiving a wash and brush up after completing its days duty before being parked up for the night.

Two more brand new buses joined the fleet in 2016, an Optare Metrocity and an Optare Solo SR. Both were delivered from Optare in all-over white livery before going to Salts at Cobridge for a repaint. YJ16 DDU (No. 165) is seen at Adderley Green depot having just been delivered on 18 June 2016.

In late December 2016 Centrebus purchased three former Tower Transit dual-door Enviro 200 single deckers and loaned them to D&G Bus for a few months. They received temporary fleet numbers 1–3 during their stay. They received D&G fleet names and numbers on their existing London red livery. YX12 AON (No. 2) is seen at Brookwood Drive Meir working a 10 from Hanley to Meir Square.

Optare Solo YJ08 PJV (No. 50) is seen here at Nantwich bus station after working rural route 73 from Audlem through local villages in September 2016. It still wears the livery of its former owner Courtney Coaches of Bracknell but received a repaint into D&G red livery shortly afterwards.

Apart from one that was withdrawn following a collision with a tree at Crewe, all of the former Bakerbus Wright Streetlite WF buses continue to earn their living working from Crewe depot. MX60 GWB (No. 153) is seen at Congleton working a 315 to Rode Heath, a regular route for these buses that was once worked by Stanways.

Optare Versa YJ57 XWB (No. 158) is seen on the Park Lane Estate at Biddulph after receiving the refreshed 'D&G Yellow 9' livery when the route was again extended from Newcastle to Clayton Westbury Park. It was one of five acquired from Transdev Burnley & Pendle in 2015 to upgrade the former Bakerbus route.

All five of the former Transdev Burnley & Pendle Optare Versas painted into the 'The Nines' livery were given the rebranded 'D&G Yellow 9' livery shortly before the route was extended back to Westbury Park from Newcastle, and with the route now requiring six buses again another Versa too received the livery. YJ57 XVZ (No. 160) is seen at Westbury Park.

The four original buses that ran the 'Orange One' were rebranded as 'D&G Orange 1' when the route was extended to Silverdale and Wood Lane. Enviro 200 SN11 FFU (No. 111) is seen here working the 1A variant to Audley and Wood Lane at Bignall End shortly after the changes.

When the 'Orange One' was extended from Newcastle to Silverdale and Wood Lane and rebranded as the 'D&G Orange 1' three more buses were required to operate the new service. Enviro 200 YX60 DXK (No. 119) is seen here at Alsagers Bamk on its way back from Wood Lane, This bus was previously yellow and in 'The Nines' livery but had also worked for D&G Bus in white livery too.

D&G Bus Optare Solo YJ56 WUV (No. 114) was repainted into the refreshed 'D&G Orange 1' livery when the route was extended from Newcastle to Silverdale and Wood Lane in 2018. It is seen at Longton bus exchange working a 1 to Meir Square.

Two former London dual-door Alexander Dennis Enviro 200 single deckers were acquired from Ensignbus in 2018 . They had been new to First Centrewest. YX09 FKW (No. 51) is seen at Adderley Green shortly after repaint. It initially worked at Adderley Green but was later transferred to Chaserider at Cannock.

Seven Alexander Dennis Enviro 200 single deckers were purchased from Ensignbus, Purfleet, in 2018 to replace older buses in the fleet. YX09 FMO (No. 43) is seen at Adderley Green depot shortly after arriving from Essex still in ex-London condition before repaint and the fitting of electronic blinds.

YX09 FMO (No. 43) the same bus in the previous photo is seen after a repaint into D&G Bus livery and the fitting of electronic blinds. It is seen standing in for a blue bus on the 'Blue 2' at Westbury Park in the rain.

Shortly after the launch of the 'Blue 2' route between Birches Head and Westbury Park Enviro 200 YX09 FME (No. 38) is seen at Westbury Park in May 2018. The bus was new to First Centrewest, London.

Alexander Dennis Enviro 200 YX09 FMF (No. 39) is seen here in original condition when the 'Blue 2' ran from Birches Head to Westbury Park via the Festival Park. It is seen here waiting time at Stafford Avenue, Clayton, on its way to Westbury Park.

Occasionally the 'Blue 2'-liveried Enviro 200s managed to wander onto other routes instead of the staying on the 2. YX09 FMF (No 39) is seen here at Fegg Hayes working a 94 from Congleton to Newcastle.

The last of the four Alexander Dennis Enviro 200s that received 'Blue 2' livery, YX09 FMM (No. 42), seen here at Birches Head when the route ran through to Westbury Park, is the only one left in this livery now that the route only runs from Hanley to Birches Head so only needs the one bus.

A batch of six Optare Versas that had been new in 2008 were purchased in early 2019 from Transdev Yellow Buses, Bournemouth. Unusually they kept their select registrations after sale to D&G Bus. Adderley Green and Crewe depots were allocated three buses each. T21 TYB (No. 21) is seen at Adderley Green still in Bournemouth yellow with silver relief.

Another of the Transdev Yellow Buses Optare Versas seen at Adderley Green depot before repaint is T25 TYB (No. 25), this time in Bournemouth yellow with blue relief. Some of these buses entered service in this condition before going for a repaint.

All but one of the Transdev Yellow Buses Optare Versas eventually received standard D&G Bus red livery. T28 TYB (No. 28) was one of those allocated to Crewe and is seen here at Congleton working a 38 from Crewe to Macclesfield.

The only one of the former Transdev Yellow Buses Optare Versas not to receive standard D&G red livery was T27 TYB (No. 27), which was repainted into the 'Yellow Nines' livery, seen here soon after repaint at Chell Heath working a 9 from Biddulph to Clayton Westbury Park.

Optare Solo YJ11 OGZ (No. 116) was a second-hand purchase from Eve of Dunbar. It had leather seats and after repaint was allocated to Crewe depot. It is seen at Fegg Hayes on its way back to Crewe after working the Biddulph Town service 93 with D&G Bus displayed on the destination blind.

Optare Solo SR YJ16 DDU (No. 165) was purchased new alongside three Optare Versas primarily to upgrade route 16 Hanley–Leek with brand new buses. It is seen here at St Edwards Park operating a school service from Westwood High School, Leek, to Cellarhead.

Three Optare Solo SRs were delivered new to Crewe depot in 2016 with Leighton Link branding in green for route 12 linking Brookhouse Estate to Crewe town centre and Leighton Hospital. YJ66 AOX (No. 48) is seen at Adderley Green shortly before entering service with the blind box frozen over due to the cold weather.

Optare Solo SR YJ13 HNB (No. 102) was one of a batch purchased new in 2013 with some initially in a silver and pink livery for Crewe town services, but have now received standard livery. It is seen at Trentham Lakes ready to work a 24 back to Hanley.

Following the withdrawal by First Potteries of their service 18 to the Haregate Estate at Leek, D&G provided a replacement by extending existing route 16 from Leek to Haregate. Optare Versa YJ65 EVR (No. 146), one of two purchased new in December 2015, waits time on the Haregate Estate in Leek ready to return to Hanley in July 2019.

The Stoke-on-Trent City Council-owned Cityrider-liveried Optare Versas occasionally venture out of the Stoke-on-Trent area on other services. YJ59 GHH (No. 173) is seen at St Edwards Park in Leek working on a 16 from Hanley. This bus has previously worked for First Potteries, Wardle Transport, D&G Bus and Scraggs before returning to D&G Bus.

Another Cityrider-liveried Optare Versa that has managed to escape Stoke-on-Trent is WT58 BUS (No. 171), seen here at Congleton ready to work a 94 back to Newcastle in July 2021. It carries a select registration from its Wardle Transport days. Route 94 is usually worked by an Optare Solo.

The large air horns and extra marker lights on the roof of Optare Solo YJ60 KFG (No. 131) give the game away that this was a former Go Goodwins vehicle. It was one of three purchased by D&G Bus in October 2015 and allocated to Crewe depot. It is seen here leaving Macclesfield on the 130 to Manchester Airport, a former Arriva North West route, in March 2023.

D&G Bus also purchased two Alexander Dennis Enviro 200s from Go Goodwins in 2015 and these too had the air horns and extra marker lights and were also allocated to Crewe depot. YX11 CNE (No. 121) is seen at Congleton working a 38 to Macclesfield.

Interesting purchases by D&G Bus in early 2019 were four Wright Streetlite DF single deckers from Isle of Man Transport. They arrived in their silver livery complete with Isle of Man registrations and would need to be reregistered before entering service. LMN 334K (No. 58) still shows an Isle of Man destination at Adderley Green depot shortly after arrival. It would later become DG58 BUS.

The four former Isle of Man Wright Streetlite DF buses were repainted into D&G red livery and allocated to Crewe. Three were branded up for new service 38 Macclesfield–Crewe in direct competition with Arriva. DG56 BUS (No. 56) is seen at Congleton shortly afterwards. D&G already provided the Sunday service on this route under contract to Cheshire East Council.

Wright Streetlite DG55 BUS (No. 55) is seen arriving in Congleton bus station all branded up for route 38 Macclesfield–Crewe in competition with Arriva North West in September 2019. Three of the Streetlites were branded up for the 38 with the fourth being a spare. Arriva would later close its depots and cease running buses in South Cheshire.

Three Wright Streetlite WF buses were purchased from Preston Bus in 2021 and quickly repainted and put into service from Crewe depot. BRZ 9662 (No. 59) is seen at Woodhouse Lane, Biddulph, working the 93 Biddulph town service in April 2021. All three were originally Wrightbus demonstrators before joining Preston Bus.

Only one Optare Solo was acquired with the seven other buses purchased with the Bakerbus operations from Bakers of Biddulph in January 2015. That was Slimline MX58 KZK (No. 143), seen here in D&G red livery at Trentham Lakes working works bus 14W to Hanley in August 2019.

Optare Solo SR KX14 FJY (No. 117), seen here at Bradwell working a 94 from Newcastle to Congleton in May 2021 shortly after entering service with D&G Bus, was an air-conditioned former Malta Bus vehicle which carried registration BUS 343 in Malta. Similar buses can be found in the Centrebus fleet.

KX06 APY (No. 126) was one of three Optare Solos that were transferred to D&G from Centrebus in 2000. It is seen here after a repaint deputising for an 'Orange 1' Optare Solo at Bath Road on the Park Site Estate in September 2021.

Another of the ex-Centrebus Optare Solos was MX05 ENF (No. 124), seen here after a repaint into D&G red livery working the former RML Travel and First Potteries route 2 between Hanley and Birches Head deputising for a 'Blue 2'-livered Enviro 200 at Birches Head before heading back to Hanley.

Optare Solo Slimline DX07 WFA (No. 128) joined the D&G Bus fleet from Stanways Coaches of Church Lawton after they lost the tender for route 315 Congleton–Alsager–Rode Heath, the route it was purchased new by Stanways to operate. It is seen here at Mossfield Road, Adderley Green, on its way back to the depot after working the Kidsgrove town service.

D&G Bus operated a batch of Optare Solos that were new to Landylines of Greenham for the Taunton Flyer services. YJ55 BHU (No. 140) is seen at Abbey Hulton looking rather faded and in need of a repaint while working route 43 from Baddeley Green to Hanley. This is another former First Potteries route taken on by D&G Bus.

Another Optare Solo from the former Landylines Greenham batch was YJ55 BHO (No. 138), seen here at Bradwell working a 94 from Newcastle to Congleton in March 2018. This bus was withdrawn shortly after this photo was taken after being written off following a collision with a car at Weston Coyney.

Alexander Dennis Enviro YX63 GYG (No. 108) is seen at Tean working a 32X from Hanley. This was a replacement route covering for withdrawn journeys on First Potteries route 32 Hanley–Cheadle–Tean. The bus was new as an Alexander Dennis demonstrator and was originally purchased by D&G Bus to work the 841 Stafford–Uttoxeter route.

D&G Bus Optare Solo YJ08 PJV (No. 50) is seen at Tean after arriving on a 32X from Hanley in February 2021. This was another route that was registered by D&G Bus to replace withdrawn journeys on First Potteries route 32. It was new to Europcar, Heathrow Airport, but came from Courtney Coaches, Bracknell.

Following the decision by First Potteries to discontinue the former Turners route 8A between Hanley, Brown Edge and Endon, D&G Bus registered a replacement service and to work this repainted one of the surplus 'Blue 2'-liveried Alexander Dennis Enviro 200s into a pseudo Turners brown and cream livery with scrolled fleet names.YX09 FME (No. 38) is seen at Baddeley Green on its way back to the depot after finishing a duty on the 8A.

A second former First London Alexander Dennis Enviro 200 to receive the Turners livery was YX09 FMF (No. 39) when the Hanley–Brown Edge–Endon route 8A was doubled in frequency to half hourly with one running to Brown Edge Schools as the 8B instead of Endon. It is seen here at Norton Green in August 2019. Note the more brown front panel on this bus.

Plaxton Pointer-bodied Dennis Dart MPD CHZ 8960 (No. 176) was the first brand new bus purchased by D&G Bus in 2004 as DK54 KKY. It is seen at Adderley Green garage in D&G red livery in April 2018 shortly before its repaint into the original blue and cream livery and regaining its original fleet number 10, which it lost when the Longton depot operations of D&G Bus were sold to Wardle Transport in 2011, becoming 176 when they were repurchased in 2015.

Plaxton Pointer-bodied Dennis Dart MPD CHZ 8960 (No. 10) was the first brand new bus purchased by D&G Bus in 2004 as DK54 KKY. It was repainted into the original blue and cream livery and regained its original fleet number 10 in 2018 to celebrate twenty years of D&G Buses. It is seen here at Congleton in September 2021 working a 94 to Newcastle. It carries a memorial on the side to the founders David Reeves and Gerald Henderson.

D&G Bus purchased three dual-door-bodied Wright Streetlite DF single deckers in late 2020 for use on the Chaserider services at Cannock from 10 January 2021. SN64 CVM (No. 64) is seen at Adderley Green depot in December 2020 newly repainted but with the lower part of the livery the wrong colour. This bus was new to Tower Transit as WV 46108 working Transport for London contracts.

Eight Wright Eclipse Urban-bodied Volvo B7RLEs were included in the deal to purchase the Cannock depot operations from Arriva Midlands in January 2021. FJ58 HYT (No. 194) is seen here at Stafford in April 2021 working an 825 to Lichfield still in Arriva livery but with Chaserider stickers and fleet numbers. It would later be repainted red at Cannock depot.

Chaserider inherited ten Plaxton Pointer-bodied Dennis Darts with the purchase of the Arriva Midlands depot at Cannock. The only one that was in the latest Arriva pale blue livery was FJ54 OTT (No. 8), seen here leaving Stafford on a 7 for Moss Pit in April 2021 with Chaserider stickers. None of these Darts survived long enough to be painted red, although some did transfer to Select Bus Services and were repainted in their livery.

D&G Bus purchased two Alexander Dennis Enviro 200MMCs from Whitelaws of Stonehouse, Scotland, for the Chaserider operations at Cannock. YX65 RWL (No. 2) remains in white livery when seen here in Cannock working a 3 to Brownhills in May 2023. These were the first MMC variants in the fleet.

The other Enviro 200MMC purchased from Whitelaws of Stonehouse, YX65 RWK (No. 1), initially worked in plain white livery for a while before receiving the standard Chaserider red livery. It is seen at Cannock after working in on a 70 from Wolverhampton in May 2023.

Chaserider inherited eight Wright Eclipse Urban-bodied Volvo B7RLEs from Arriva Midlands with the purchase of the Cannock operations in January 2021. All received the Chaserider livery as seen here on FJ58 HYV (No. 196) at Cannock bus station in May 2023 with a 25 Pye Green Circular. This was formerly Arriva Midlands 3911.

Six Alexander Dennis Enviro 200MMC buses in the Chaserider fleet wear this attractive silver, orange and maroon livery with Travel Telford fleet names to operate tendered services in the Telford area, but on 24 May 2023 YX22 OGG (No 540) has managed to stray onto a 25 Pye Green Circular service at Cannock bus station.

Several youthful second-hand buses were acquired by D&G Bus to join some of the former Arriva buses with the Cannock operations in January 2021. One was Alexander Dennis Enviro 200 YN62 AOH (No. 24), seen here in Stafford working a 74 to Cannock. This bus was new to Littles of Derby for the Pride Park park and ride service but came to D&G Bus from Ensignbus. It has since transferred to the D&G fleet at Adderley Green.

At the time of writing only one of the handful of Wright Commander-bodied DAF SB220s inherited from Arriva Midlands with the purchase of the Cannock operations in January 2021 survives in service. FJ06 ZTK (No. 187) is seen at Cannock ready to depart on a 25 Pye Green Circular service. Not many of these buses survived long enough to receive Chaserider red livery, most being transferred to Select Bus Services in Arriva livery before repaint. The bus still has the dodgy blind it had in Arriva days.

Chaserider Wright Streetlite DF FN63 KFL (No. 611), seen here in Cannock working a 62 to Lichfield, is one of two buses in the fleet wearing a black all-over advert for Cannock Chase Radio. They were both new to Isle of Man Transport before joining the Centrebus fleet. This bus was formerly registered LWN 441K.

Optare Metrocity YJ17 FXE (No. 799) was new as an Optare demonstrator before being purchased by Centrebus and allocated to Leicester. It was later transferred to the Chaserider operation at Cannock and is seen at Cannock bus station working a 74 to Stafford still in Centrebus colours but with Chaserider fleet names attached in May 2023.

Two Optare Metrocity buses were acquired in late 2021 that had been new to APH and used as airport parking buses. One of these was YJ67 GBY (No. 151) seen here at Adderley Green Garage in January 2022 in plain white livery and still in original condition with only twenty-four seats and extra large luggage pens. They would later go to the Cannock bodyshop to be upseated and repainted but did enter service at Cannock for a short period in this condition before the work was completed.

The other former APH airport parking Optare Metrocity was YJ67 GBX (No. 149), seen here looking immaculate in August 2022 at Meir Square while working a 1 to Park Site. This was shortly after it had returned to service at Adderley Green from Cannock following work to remove the extra large luggage pens, increasing the seating capacity from twenty-four seats to forty-four and a repaint into standard D&G red livery.

Optare Versa YJ62 FSS (No. 781) is seen here at Mossfield Road, Adderley Green, on its way back to the depot after working a 32X to Tean in May 2022. It was one of two such vehicles to join the fleet from Centrebus-owned High Peak. They initially worked in High Peak green livery before a repaint into D&G red. It had been new to Travel de Courcey, Coventry.

Following the extra work taken on with the closure of the Arriva depots at Macclesfield and Winsford, significantly more buses would be required to operate all these extra replacement services. Some were transferred from Centrebus but others were sourced from elsewhere such as Optare Solo SR YD63 UZH (No. 297), one of a pair arriving from Ross Travel of Featherstone and initially working in their blue and white livery with D&G fleet names. 297 is seen in Congleton in May 2023 working a 42 to Crewe.

Enviro 200 YX16 OHW (No. 4) was one of two buses that received a special red and yellow livery with branding for route 84X Crewe–Nantwich direct that ran in competition with Stagecoach on the former Arriva route 84 between the two towns. It is seen here at Nantwich in June 2023 and was new to TLC Travel, West Bowling. The Stagecoach 84 ran from Crewe to Chester.

Six Alexander Dennis Enviro 200s were transferred from Centrebus to D&G Bus in April 2023 and allocated to Crewe to operate the replacement services following the withdrawal of all the Arriva services in the area with the closure of their garages at Macclesfield and Winsford. One of these was YY64 GWG (No. 532), seen at Congleton on former Arriva route 38 Crewe–Macclesfield three days after the changes took place. It carries the new Centrebus orange and blue livery.

Another new addition to the fleet after the Arriva North West garage closures was Alexander Dennis Enviro 200 YX16 ODJ (No. 91), which worked in white livery but with D&G fleet names. It is seen at Congleton Fairground with a 42 to Crewe via Holmes Chapel in June 2023. This bus was new to Menzies Aviation at Heathrow Airport and had a computer-operated manual transmission.

In early 2023 two Enviro 200s were exchanged with High Peak for two Optare Solo SRs needed at Buxton due to long-term roadworks. Following the extra work taken on after the Arriva garage closures in Cheshire these buses eventually became permanent members of the fleet and received repaints into D&G red livery. YY64 GWM (No. 594) is seen at Fegg Hayes while working a 9 to Hanley but is still displaying Chaserider on the blind after being repainted at Cannock.

One of the highlights of 2023 was the repainting of Alexander Dennis Enviro 200 YX63 LGG (No. 504) into North Western Road Car livery to celebrate the centenary of the formation of North Western in 1923. Many of the routes taken over after the Arriva garage closures in Cheshire were former North Western routes. It is seen here at Knutsford working an 88 from Macclesfield to Altrincham.

Three Alexander Dennis Enviro 200MMCs were acquired from Cardiff Bus in late 2023 and allocated to the Macclesfield depot primarily to work Macclesfield town services 3 to Weston and 10 to Bollington. CN17 BHD (No. 571) leaves Macclesfield bus station with a 3 to Weston shortly after entering service.

Four brand new MCV Evora-bodied Volvo B8RLE buses were delivered to Chaserider in early 2024 to upgrade former Arriva service 60 from Cannock to Lichfield. Two were painted in Standard D&G red livery but the other two introduced a new livery with a blue rear seperated by a diagonal yellow band. BV73 MJX (No. 640) is seen at Cannock working a 60 to Lichfield in red livery.

The new D&G Bus livery is seen on MCV Evora-bodied Volvo B8RLE BV73 MKE (No. 639) at Lichfield bus station working a 60 back to Cannock. It is an adaptation of the new Centrebus livery but with red replacing the Centrebus orange and the dividing line in yellow instead of white.

Existing vehicles were gradually repainted in the new livery when repainting was necessary, usually after accident damage. Optare MetroCity YJ67 GBX (No. 149) shows off the new livery at Adderley Green depot after accident damage repairs at the Cannock bodyshop following a collision with a bus stop at Fegg Hayes.

New additions to the fleet were usually painted into the new livery before entering service. Enviro 200 YX18 KYF (No. 524) is seen at Newchapel working a Sunday 7 from Kidsgrove to Hanley, a service run by First Potteries the rest of the week. This bus had worked briefly in white livery and had been used by First Bus at East Midlands Airport.

More brand new buses delivered in late 2023 were four Alexander Dennis Enviro 200MMCs for Crewe depot. Three were forty seaters to upgrade former Arriva service 38 from Crewe to Macclesfield, with the other a shorter thirty-four-seater version for town service 8 to Sydney. YY73 RFE (No. 575) is seen arriving at Sandbach working a 38 from Macclesfield to Crewe.

All of the Alexander Dennis Enviro 200MMCs were delivered in the D&G Bus red livery but YY73 REU (No. 574) suffered accident damage when a car ran into the back of it when it was a few weeks old. It received the new livery following repairs at Cannock bodyshop. It is seen at Congleton shortly afterwards working a 38 to Macclesfield.

The latest new buses delivered to D&G Bus in August 2024 were further MCV Evora-bodied Volvo B8RLEs for Adderley Green depot. These were delivered in a yellow version of the new livery with 'The Nines' branding for the 9 Biddulph–Clayton. BP24 UJA (No. 6003) is shown at Church Road, Biddulph, during its first week in service.